you.

/juː/

pronoun

all about

number three in the trilogy

two minute poems

written daily, almost, and all on @threads.

similar

me, i, he, she, thee, pity

Haider Bahrani

i

mongrelhybrid.com

to
dad
wish you could read them

Contents

*volume 3 in the two minute poems trilogy originally
written on micro blogging site @threads each a little bit
of the day's story presented in reverse chronology*

*each was written and these were my rules ad hoc and in
less than a minute or two with some light touch editing
mostly in the first five minutes and a little bit as i put
them together here for you*

as you can tell i've left out the punctuation mostly

that i will leave up to you

the first line of nearly all is the title too

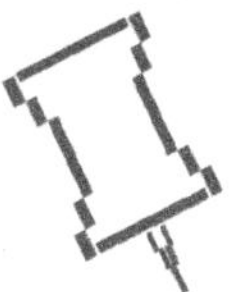

pinned thread

when i start
a bit of verse on here
i have no idea
what i will write next
nor the context
nor when
i end

this is at the start of each volume

YOU

you
the one
you think about
the most
my obsession
this is
my confession
you
the centre
of your attention
burdened
not free
me
in thought
and in reflection
is all
the i
can see

it's a conspiracy
don't believe a word
they are after something
what they are selling
is absurd
it doesn't fit
with their normal pattern
and they are lying
to make what they want happen
they've tidied their bedrooms
they've put away their shoes
they were even nice to each other
that's definitely new
i tell you what too
they paid attention
when i asked them to do
so i tell you
there is a plan afoot
but if i give them what they want
if i relent
they'll go back to their ways
that groan
that moan
that look

poetry
the dreams
of the young
of mostly love
and songs
of want
want
want
cries for justice
for the war torn
and mistreated
chickens
then
they get older
at least they vote more
but they morn less
for the people
than their dogs
and their kittens

limited
the information we get
it never seems
enough
yet
spirited
we carry on
it's tough
and we mostly guess
well it could be
just me
yes
this is another poem
about playing my daughter
at monopoly

late night write
words written
not in the light
can you see?
the might
of them
is as bright
as the desert
sunlight

*in reply to my own, "it's not" see
p13*

a surprise
why plan
when it's always
the next thing
not quite
as expected?
to realise
sooner that life
really is more
less according to plan
reactive
and to prepare
if we can
from that
perspective

it's not
that i
don't
or won't
i just can't
because
i shan't
be able
and you need
something
or someone
more stable
perhaps too
more capable
i flitter
though not
a quitter
you'll find
my distraction
distracting
my forever
meandering
will have you
constant
in a state of
wondering
what on earth
and when
things
if ever
might be happening
though
i am sure

all [the] balls
i am juggling
will at
some point be
landing

in beta mode
it's always the case
when you are on
that creative road
it's a never ending race
you're carrying all the load
and the only one
making the pace
then all of a sudden
you're done
but you know
it's not really
this bit here
and that one
could be better
clearly
if someone
says it's surely finished
the look on my face!

fallow day
few words
to say
i'm out
to play
music
today

the perfect
picture
curated
painted
to be feted
the hunger
to be adored
is just another way
to be incarcerate

society
it has expectations
it has a comment
to make about
all your flirtations
usually from just
a few members whose view
is their society
may not be for you
i mean maybe that's true
who would want
to be amongst
those who have
so little better to do?

cooking
if i sit here
any longer
i'll be ready
for eating
here am i bleating
as i did
when it was raining
for which i am now
praying

arg!
of not if
my smelling whiffs
i was in a rush
in between
two bouts of fuss
i feel a need
to cuss

i'm halfway
done
but nowhere near finished
this used to be
something i cherished
it was once fun
but if i
eat one more bite
of this scone
i think a button
or two
may come undone

i saw the future
but then it passed
really fast
and i just threw away
the last of it
i missed the next two
as i was just getting to grips
with my current
new new
as they went passed me
even faster
and before i knew it
what i have now
is three things older
than the new new
new new

silence
well sort of
the road in the distance
the vague sound
of a train
on a far away track
clickety clack
clickety clack
the odd instance
of a door slam
and the growl
of an angry cat
then a lawn mower
a strimmer
a couple of neighbours
yap yap yap
then the birds
some crow
some sing
with some harmony
a cacophony
really
did i say silence?
what's that?

i look through
a window
and all i see
is tree
tree
tree
tree
with the sky
and the sun
elegantly
peering through
the branches
the leaves
this is how
the earth once was
apparently
and perhaps
how it should
be

a losing streak
the winner
every time
well that used to be
me
it was a matter of fact
and it was
dare i say
easy
but now
i have to hand over
that crown
as i watch my daughter smile
as she now
wins
every time
at monopoly

it's a quandary
i have to get it all
but i only really
need a bit of it
i'd say put it aside
one day
i'll use the rest of it
but that
and i know it
is a lie
it'll take up space
and someone will find it
not quite sure
what to do with it
when i die

does it
make you cry?
make you feel you are
alive?
is it that thing you do
that makes you
fly?
do that

just a temporary
measure
with minimal intent
as i wait for an event
which will require
my attention
so i am in contention
with all distractions
till then
breath abating
time stalling
energy sapping
oh we're on
then done
just waiting for
the next one

the

there will be
a change
soon
yes the sun
is often followed
by the moon
and sometimes
they are both in play
but that's not new
this one is novel
this one
to me at least
is big
so much so
it demands a feast
though
just in case
i'll stay tight lipped
and twice yes
i will celebrate
so
i'm having
chicken
and chips

enough
well for today
coffee for one
and yesterday
i certainly
ate too much
but definitely
i have enough
of all sorts of stuff for i am
fortunate enough

i'm running out
and here comes the sun
i'm running out
to catch some

that was
nice
i'll have another
slice
now i've done this
twice
it probably counts as
a vice
and would counter
some medical
advice
but it's my new addiction
i'm definitely
doing it
thrice

from the stalls
not from the wings
for today i mean
it can be fun
behind the scenes
every night
but it's refreshing
to watch
from the seats
as you delight
then take
the curtain call

the first three lines
because
we don't have time
it seems
so no one
excepting
a curious
or could be just a procrastinating
few
are committing the crime of reading
beyond
the header
and the next two

sour the milk
that ilk
words stir emotions cause commotion
turn happiness
into sad
sadness
into mad
but why use them
for ill?
if their happiness
makes you envious
or jealous
best keep
your lips still

tick tick tock
will someone
please turn off
the clock
tick tick tock
who needs a reminder time does not
stop?
tick tick tock
if we don't chase it
so what?

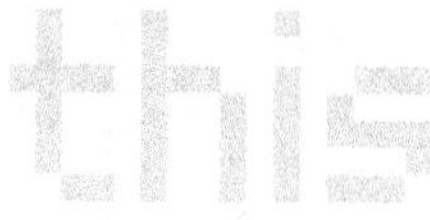

i'll check
not sure
if they are done yet
the game is on
and their game is on
for every
thing
and moment
and all the time it's on
they put on a bet
so i'll check
but they wont even notice
i've been in
i bet

i can't remember
not really
i know that clearly
and what i do recall
i am not sure
if that
is real at all
things pass
and fade
and that's just stuff
from yesterday
but the day
that one thing happened
when i was small
i remember it
definitely
and surely
maybe

it's probably
not the best
maybe even
below the rest
but today
in my kitchen
it's the only
so the one and only
i made it
enjoyed every minute
even if it is
as cakes go
a bit rocky

ah my bed
finally
a time
to rest my head
that said
let me just see
scroll down my messages
watch some tv
and oh
that's an interesting
long read
erm
right i'm going
to brush my teeth
i better go check
the kids
also just one last
oh no is that the time?
i really really must
slee...

watching
but are they really?
do i do things
because i think
people can see me?
is there such a person
with such an obsession?
i mean only i
can see me really
and no more
than i can see them
can they
nor do they care to
really see me
surely?

storm
the norm
always on the brew
not one
but a few
serenity
of mind
is the time
between thoughts
and they are becoming less too

so?
we snore
like yawning
why
is a thing
of folklore
best keep it
that way
else to dine
we would have
less to say
and seems
such a bore

44

i did it again
i wrote
the same poem
three times
since then
when
i said
rinse repeat
but then again
the rhyme
and words
were each time
new
and the beat
the rhythm
were different
too
so many
million selling lps
with 12 songs
all saying the
same thing
to 12
sometimes just 6 different tunes

done
tick
ah now i can
oh hold on
but it's not
really quite
i'll go back
and see
as it lacks
a few things
i'll fix it
hopefully
but i'm tired
and a bit wired
but maybe
before the day
is
done

is it
best
to be quiet?
sometimes
you say something
it upsets someone
they say things
life for minute
comes a little
undone
moods turn
to rainy weather
yet is it better
to live under
a fake sun?

day planned
interrupt
thought pattern
disrupt
cause of
a discourse
universe on
collision course interrupt
wipe the palms
sip a cup of calm
day replanned
phone
switched off

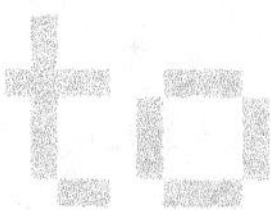

if you
don't mind
i'll wait
see what you find
then i'll
ponder it
and decide
though
the truth is
really
i've already
made my decision
and my faith
in your quest
well i don't want to be
outwardly unkind
my silence on that bit
has allowed me
wriggle space
so if by chance
you do not blunder
i can pretend
without having
to save face

a chance
find
but yes
it was placed
in my path
like so much
i don't see
but this
caught my eye
then my ear
and now it's all i hear
for today at least
the new soundtrack
of my mind

not going
to pretend
my back hurts
when i bend
knees too
when i descend
but when i run
climb
swim
any kind of fun
the pain
is gone
so i will play
till
the very
end

some 10

some none
more come
when i walk
when i run
but mostly
forgotten
by the time
i get time
to type
or write them

*to question: how many poems do you
write a day?*
by @unscripted30s on @threads

it's nice
how some of us
can be
over generous
with our advice
i say that
as in some cases
however few
it's actually true
generosity indeed
in many areas
is lacking
every day being
a school day
is a phrase
that gets my backing
but sometimes
it's wise
to take the
more quiet
advice

aha
mmm
yeah
er
erm
n'
not rea'
uhm
ok
uh
i have to
mmm
aha

you read
half the sentence
and missed out
some punctuation
so what you said
you missaid
so we have a situation
it's ok
i can forgive
it's not quite right
but we will live
next time
read out the recipe
to the letter
then what we have
with our coffee
will be
so much better

i knew
it was so obvious
yet
i behaved like
i didn't have a clue
the surprise
wasn't a surprise
to you
as you knew too
i'd swapped
the marmalade
with the chutney pickle
while tidying the cupboard
the jars look the same
so i'm to blame
i should have
left it a mess
as when
breakfast time came
well no need to guess
the obvious
came true

ah yes
you forgot
the last time
you did that
you were 25
twice that now
the kids found it funny
and you are thinking
i'm so glad
i'm still
alive

centre

i'll take
my time
stock
and a sip
from your
glass of wine
because
i'm comfortable
waiting
not for you
or someone
to slip
the medal
the throne
to hold up
a silver cup
is not a goal
or an end
i'm waiting
just for you
so we can just
sit and do
to no particular
end

cold coffee
i have it frequently
i mean doesn't everybody?
i make it hot
then the kids ask
can
is and what?
i mean
i didn't used to be
a fan
but now i've tried it
a lot!
but cold tea
definitely
not!

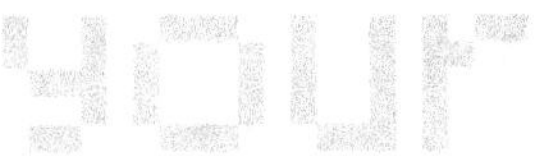

the last
one
no
not that one
the one before
you
yes
just after that
oh was it?
so
yes
the one
in between
then no
it must have been
a different one
let me look
ah this is it
oh yes
sorry
it was from
the same time
last week
and it was
the one before
the last
before we
sat down to eat
no?

with care
i think
we differ in how we
accomplish
there are ways
less selfish
even if we are not
so accomplished
in such things we do
to bother
even
for ourselves
or in the aid
or care
of others
means
i think
we do it
so much better

battery low
well down
to 20% now
if i'm human
anxious
keep looking at it
every 2 seconds and a bit
driving myself
peanuts
so
i'd charge it
immediately
only the mad ones
surely
wait till it's
zero?

in contrast
is a contrarian
hide out
when the light is on
a light
when everyone
else
is wrong
and when they are
they still
go on and on

team
pick up
where i
put down
push on as
you push off
lean in
as i lean on
team
makes work
and play
more fun

i suppose
if you strike
a moral pose
then be prepared
to be exposed

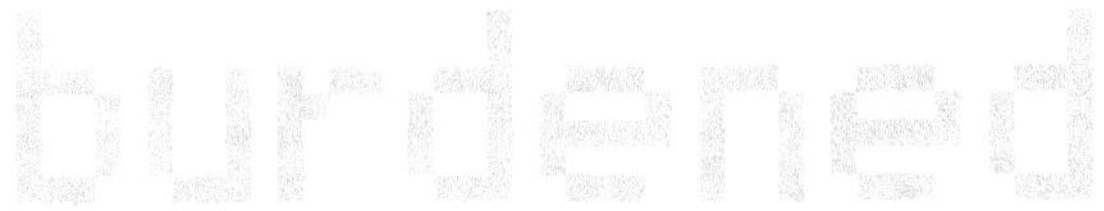

always on
a mission
won't
or don't
have time
to listen
to voices
of differing
thought
and reason
going nowhere
like most of us
human

they call it revolution
because it keeps
coming back the same
it's touted as a solution
but it's so over used
it's inane
it seems that
all we want is change
just so everything
stays the same
the same
the same
the same

if you only have
one size hammer
and you have nails
to bang in
big and small
how are you
going to be able
to do them all?

events
as ever
push you off course
there will be those
who will kindly
keep the experts
on how to do their jobs
informed
of course
and will be
forever
chasing this cause

i have been influenced
obviously
by all i hear and see
that's not a choice
we make
and it's a school
that comes for free
but if i am
under the influence
it's where i once chose to be
please use your influence
if it's a place you ever find me

if it makes you happy
if it doesn't hurt anyone
is it that easy?
is it knowingly
as long as it's not
hurt out of jealousy?
or if it makes you happy
and don't get
caught out
is that what it's
all about?
or is it even
more complicated
than that?
if it makes you happy
and it's hurting you
then maybe that's
just a ruse
if it makes you happy
later makes you sad
a temporary fix
you use
asking these questions
makes us
well me
even more confused
if it makes you happy
i can say
i'm glad

oh well i think
i got away with that
i'll make it look like
it was all part of the plan
but i'll keep that
under my hat
don't tell me
it's not what you
sometimes do
i know you wing it
often too
20 years of practice
and paying attention
at school
makes things
just come
easier to you

the rules
are rules
yet weirdly
as it may be
to rule a sentence
or rhyme
without much doubt
some words
and they must
commit a crime

hands in the earth
witness
to another birth
sunshine
and let's hope it rains
just enough
to green this turf
to bless the view
i'll be doubling up
on that hope
for daisies
dandelions
and buttercups
too

that was fun
chit chat
this n that
kids playing
with a real ball
and bats
if we take
our eyes off
could become
rare that

if it's complex
i think
it'd better be good
because simple
songs on a loop
are everyday food
unless it's your
science
fetish
or hobby
you study
it'll leave us all
perplexed
so it better be
better than
an ivor novello
or bohemian rhapsody

pending
pretty much
everything
it's a bit like
the universe
it's mostly
hydrogen
if we round it up
life
is just
waiting

download
and clear
but it's not ever gone
take it to a good fixer
and it doesn't take them long
it all reappears
all hail the good fixer
unless
we want it all to disappear

sleep
my lover
i promise
you'll have
me and
my devotion
for longer
my eyes
barely open
i feel
without remiss
i could be
with you
forever

in a rush
to do
well
things
i told you about lists
but i don't have time
not to read them
not even for this
so i better get on
just after
i've had this coffee
and a bag of crisps

lists
we like them
actually we hate them
but yes we like them
we make so many
it drives us
well me
potty
then lists of lists
then post-its
and then we do
what we need to do
usually without much ado
well not with all
the do do
the lists created
for you!
and you know
you know
it's true

on track
definitely
well i'll be honest
there has been
at least one
set back
but we are wading
through the forest
and we'll be fine
i'm pretty sure
as our publicist says
we'll be
on time

a person of integrity
by that
what i really mean
is someone like me
however
and who
i might be?
i do not see myself
not as i see you
neither in reflection
am i truly true
there may be
in fact certainly
some distortion
in my point of view

picking up
where i left off
but i left off
a while back
then
events
took me off track
a journey
through a land
where every dawn
has a new sun
some shine
some burn
and hope lives
when the rain comes

what if?
i mean
there's a lot of that
some reasonable
others
well
it will never
come to that
but crazy times
have come
made themselves
at home
are seasonable
and for that
they make media hosts
and newspaper moguls
fat

so sure of it
the answer i gave
to that question
but you never asked it
you have that something
that looks interesting
and i had this urge
to pretend
i know something about it
and did you know
and yes i can explain
because i read
or was it i saw?
this fifteen second clip
about it

eras end

some go down
the straight pipe
others take the bend
waters anew
or slowly curing glue
whatever the next phase
it too
will one day
be erased

the master
well i fooled
myself
maybe them
for a moment
i think
actually
if anyone noticed
it was quite a disaster
i'd fried an egg
so i thought
i could bake
but when it cooled
it was so flat
'twas like i cooked it in a pan
i'll stick to eggs
perhaps try toast
hereinafter

raw

garlic
in the raw
pleasure
the palette
and the flesh
when we press
for i am
guilty of
this lust
i must
confess

don't call me
shorty
i say often
jokingly
ad infinitum
probably
annoyingly
but i've also said
we repeat
repeatedly
now i've just
got to go do
that thing
i do every morning
so
see you shortly

there will be tears
there's not enough
stuff to go round
and as we're
passing them about
some are taking two
and a few
more than that too
then we get to
the end of the queue
the last few
we break them in two
and still
the last one
gets none
we have realised
our fears
maybe we should
have thought better
what to do?

i shouldn't have started
i was looking
for something
i knew it was
probably
in with those things
but then i stumbled
upon other somethings
and curiosity
got some seeds planted
and they grew rapidly
they blossomed
and fruited
so much i had to make
crumbles
pies
freeze some
i mean i'm up to my eyes
i was looking
for something
it's not in with those things
not that i can find
maybe it's with those
other things
put to the side?

i've put it
in a box
with my favourite
old socks
with a pack
of rare chews
and a pair
of cool shoes
i wore
when i was
new
to all the things
we do
when we
have to
without the hold
of a grown up hand
[with]
a reminder
of them
[which]
when i
with luck
grow old
will
be caught up
tangled
for me to find
[it]
inside those
socks

thump

thump
thump
thump thump
thump thump thump
thump thump thump thump
thump thump
thump
hhhhhuuuh
thump
hhhhuuuhhhh
thump
mmmuuuuhh
hhhuuuhhhh
thump

the spontaneous
launch
of a mind rocket
goes
wherever
the weather takes it

not as expected
but needs must
we had a list
and by the time
it was writ
it no longer fit
into the way
we now must
grasp this day

in awe
of the words
the scores
written
i am so smitten
those who write
wonderfully
are many many
lyric
prose
music too
yet we cheer
but a few

if i rhyme
rhyme with
rhyme
and you
with you
does it mean
my verse
is only worth
flushing
down the
loo?

two minutes
yes?
i'll be with you
yes just
two
yes please
hold on
just give me one
yes just
hang on
i just need
yup
one sec
i've just got to do
i'll be with you
a moment
two minutes
i can give
so

it would be
an embarrassment
to have constant
adulation
luckily
i don't

i have to
it's an obligation
but only one i have
put on myself
so you could say i don't
but it's a situation
that could
by stealth
lead to frustration
as i've found
myself out

determined
and
i'm sure of it
for the next thing
will happen
and i won't be
distracted one bit
i'll just make that coffee
read the news
i'm sure i needed
to clean
those muddy shoes
tea bags
did we run out of tea bags?
i'm sure i didn't
put them on the list
oh look how those trees
are blowing
in the wind

with nothing
we leave
so don't bother
throwing in
anything
they'll just hug
the worms
like the earth
and the leaves
and they are
anyway
best left
for those who
are left
with memories
to enjoy
the reminiscing
and to keep
dancing
singing
the songs
and writing
your lines
as and not
before
you go on
and promise
as much as you can
to keep going
on and on
then
when it comes
hand it on
as with nothing
you will be gone

wait
till it's all done
to do that other one
but hold on
what if it's never
goes on forever
battle that's
never won?

reflection

an open
wound
clean it up
and put on
a plaster
it'll be fine
no big disaster
but if you leave it
so busy
you
forget to clean it
a simple thing
festering
could mean
no more
after

it's for sale
i made it up
it pushes all the buttons
to make you feel you
like you always did
and do
so hurry up
as tomorrow
like today
without fail
the price
goes up

two minutes of it
on some
maybe five
of the day
you almost
won't notice
but one hundred
in a row
and slowly slowly
it grows
and this thing
you are doing
or by then even
done
is alive
so without it feeling a chore
without fanfare
or notice
you built something
bigger and with more than
you'd ever believe or dare
and you did this
bit by bit

you got me
you caught me out
i've been faking it
and now you know
there's no doubt
the ultimate imposter
so you can roster
me out
of your routine
whatever your plans were
i can't promise you anything
i wouldn't take the risk
not with me
but you'll be ok
you've got this
you seem so good at it
just don't say
all this time
you've been
winging it
just like me!

it's in hand
i say that
i had a plan
but like all plans
before you start
it's already
down the pan
what and whatever
it is before us
is not constant
nor was it ever before
despite my reminiscence
yet
as i said
it is in hand
from what i recall
and understand

self
esteem
worth
worship
hate
pity
ish
centred
absorbed
doubt
destructive
aware
made
motivated
assured
less
contained
it's the
all
we are about

just here
just talking
coffee
tea
at the local café
they know what we drink
without even asking
unloading the week
sometimes on repeat
bouncing off the mood
but it's always good
just to be
here
with friends
just
talking

i did it already
i could have waited
till i was
y'know
ready
but i know
and some of you
you too know
i'd never be
as you say
ready
so i just did it
didn't over think it
already
and i'll
do it again
before
i think
i'm ready

i'm sure
it's no longer
winter
but if i'd
woken up
from a coma
today
i wouldn't guess
by the weather
i digress
as ever

some we nod
others we say
good morning
and hello
but for some
we stop
we chat
without
measure of time
as we talk about
this and that
some
on some days

straight
from the maker
they say
but they squeeze
them hard
till they squeak
so we can get them
cheap
cheap
cheap

if it's
raining fire
how can you hope
to aspire?

response from @nona80_swanette
By hunkering down
In metal attire
Until the storm passes
And reveals your desire
#CallAndResponse

my reply

hope alone
is all we seek
the storm has made us
hungry and meek
there are very few left
here
made of iron

colour

every turn
of my head
spring
is up
and out of bed
brushed it's teeth
combed its hair
looking good
with all its glare
holler the birds
warn the worms
the yellows
the reds
the flowers
the shades of green
of the trees
and ferns
spring
is here
did you hear?
pop on a hat
pull up a chair

i must declare
i have borne witness
events so unseemly
yet as much as i
have been disgruntled
i have in turn
done little
to bring attention to
or to overturn
for i
or we even
can talk and
put on a show
but the prevailing wind
will forever
against us
blow

the connection
it's hard to know
if and when
it's going to happen
it's hard to tell
if you made it or
[you] threw a coin
into a well
it still arrives
unexpected
a warm gust
in a windy chill
and the course
from now on
for you at least
is redirected

exposure
to the masses
can be like time in the cold
the adulation
the indifference
or worse
maybe it's truly blissful
to be totally ignored
a tortured poet
knows this
as this is their muse
for even happiness
makes them blue
success is suffering
to them
as much as to have nothing
feeding their purpose
with words
and words
anew

it used to take an age
for a thing
to become old hat
yet this verse
like much
before it's even done
is already
at that stage
even before i say the word
that

i'm waiting
for my bus
he said
to that voice
in his head
two have come
one standing
one just gone
neither of which
i wish to get on
there is another
just in view
i'll wait and see if
i just
let it pass through

everybody is
doing
talking
taking
being
feeling it
and so
i suppose
must i
why?

it's an original
i wear it proud
i'm an individual
i shout it out loud
i want to stand out
looking just like
everyone else
in my crowd

it's complicated
he said
as he lay there
staring
into the emptiness
of all the things there
simply thinking
for and with
what there is left
to think with
taking the last turn
into the last road
is this all there is?
it's complicated
and simply so

the forever
war
the love affair
we have
with
sharp focus
on what are
in our eyes
our failings
our faults
the serum
the therapy
the next season's
clothes
the fix
the fix
it's not just
politics
we are
forever
sold

we think we won
and we did
this one
but what they did
they knew
what we'd do
how we'd react
the victory we'd claim
so what's their game?
we think it's us
but what if
they're
the smarter ones?

i just put it down
right here
in front of me
all i did
was go to the loo
and make a cup of tea
where else could it be?
i've checked in the bathroom
the kitchen
and all over my desk
i don't actually need it
but if i don't find it
my mind won't rest

i am none the wiser
yes indeed
i sat through it
everything
every bit
i bet you a fiver
and you know i don't bet
it's a fools gambit
that you wouldn't
if you heard it
and sat right through it
like i did
either

braun
yes it wins
a lot
but the whole war
it will not be won
by a big brute
weighing two tons
but by the smart
maybe to some eyes
not so beautiful
or handsome
brainy
one

if everything we do
is a sell
where is our soul?
if everything we do
is to appeal
how are we whole?
the hole
that is marked
the one that
we long to fill
the time that passes
when we are
too busy
too tired
or ill
then when
the time comes
we find ourselves
tired again
and too old
so we hope
for our children
to fill their own
but then
their time passes
as well